THE RIVERTEST

A PAINTER'S JOURNEY FROM SOURCE TO SEA

BRYAN DUNLEAVY

THE RIVER TEST

A Painter's Journey from Source to Sea

Published by Magic Flute Publications 2015

ISBN 978-1-909054-14-1

Copyright © Bryan Dunleavy

Magic Flute Publications is an imprint of

Magic Flute Artworks Limited

231 Swanwick Lane

Southampton SO31 7GT

www.magicfluteartworks.com

A catalogue description of this book is available from the British Library

Contents

The River

In my boyhood growing up in Buckinghamshire I went through a phase of being very interested in fishing. In that part of the world that meant coarse fishing but I became aware, although I did not actually see, any fly fishing. Such activities were the domain of fisherman on the River Test which was said to be one of the finest trout streams in the country. How true that was I could not say because at that age I was inclined to accept most things uncritically. However, I did read a cartoon strip in the Daily Mirror, called 'Mr Crabtree Goes Fishing', written and drawn by a man called Bernard Venables, who was able to instruct young people in the art of angling. His published book became a best seller, and Venables was almost a household name in those days.

Forty years later I did get my first sight of the River Test, and indeed of fly fishermen in waders standing in the middle of the stream flicking their lures expertly onto the water, and one could stand on a bridge and watch the trout through the clear water swimming through the bright stream. My boyish passion for fishing never carried over into adulthood so I have no mature experiences to discuss, but I do remember those quiet days

beside the River Ouse with a long pole hanging over the bank.

The River Test rises from springs near the village of Ashe cuts a westwards stream to Whitchurch, where it turns south to Stockbridge, gathering strength and volume as it descends the valley. At Stockbridge it opens up into a wide flat bottomed valley with several streams and channels. These streams continue to Romsey and beyond, where the activity of man has created irrigation ditches and overflow channels.

Finally the river opens into an estuary between Redbridge and Totton. Much land has been reclaimed

1

on the Southampton side for docks and industrial purposes and at the Southampton peninsula the river merges with the Itchen into Southampton Water.

Along this journey of some 40 miles the main river is fed by tributaries. The Bourne joins the river just below Whitchurch; the Dever straggles from the east until it joins the mainstream at Chilbolton, and the Anton, which begins its life north of Andover and is itself joined by a stream from the Anna Valley, feeds into the main river near Fullerton. Wallop Brook and the Sombourne Stream join the river above Mottisfont. Finally, two more rivers add their waters where the River Dun meets at Mottisfont and the River Blackwater at Testwood.

Romsey is probably the largest settlement on the river, which for most of its length is spotted with small villages. The only industry belonging to the river are the former mills, none of which, with the part-time exceptions of the Whitchurch Silk Mill and the Eling Tide Mill, are now-working mills. Many had historical significance. The valley is still used for farming and watercress beds can be found in abundance in some stretches. Fishing retains its importance and in season fishermen come from all parts to try to lure the trout and the grayling.

Two antique caravans discovered above Overton.

The river springs from this pool near Ashe.

Source

The river has its visible source close to the tiny village of Ashe in northern Hampshire. It is an area quite free from urban development, although, up to about 150 years ago, it supported a rural population of several hundred. Certainly in the time of Jane Austen, who lived a few miles away at Steventon, the parish could support a rector in some comfort from the income of the land. The former rectory, which has been in private hands since 1907, remains as a record of those times.

The rectory and church at Ashe has a tangential connection to Jane Austen. She became good friends with the rector's wife, Mrs Lefroy, and there is a suggestion that Jane had a romance with her nephew, Tom Lefroy. Whether this mutual attraction developed very far we do not know, but it would not have led to marriage. Tom Lefroy was dependent upon the patronage of a rich uncle and would be expected to bring money into the family through marriage. Jane Austen, who was by no means from a poor family, did not have the resources to make a good catch. If she was to marry at all, it would be to a vicar, such as Mr.

The early course of the river stream. Below: Quidhampton Mill.

Elton in her book Emma, rather than to a great landowner like Mr. Darcy. Fiction was so much more satisfying than fact,

No doubt this fed material into her novels. The Lefroys, who descended from a Huguenot family with Portal associations, held the living of Ashe for three generations. One of the Lefroys, born here in 1817, was part of the detail which dug up Napoleon's body at St Helena in 1840 so that it could be transferred to a tomb in Paris.

The church at Ashe - not as old as it looks.

And this village has further literary connections. The mother of Mary Russell Mitford, the Berkshire writer, grew up in this rectory and of course knew the Austens.

The church is relatively new. Although there was a church on this site at the time of Domesday, the 12th century building and its 14th century additions were almost completely obliterated during the building of the new church in 1877-8.

The underground springs that feed the river well up into a large pool just to the west of the old rectory. I spoke to the man who allowed me to walk across his field and he told me that the level of the pool varies seasonally, but it is enough to start the river in a narrow winding channel as it flows downhill. Ashe is about 500 feet above sea level.

The water breaks into a narrow silvery stream that winds its way towards Quidhampton where the force of the water is powerful enough to drive the first mill on the Test. Not far away the industrial chimneys

A view from The Greyhound down Overton's Winchester Street. The village is laid out with fairly wide through streets.

Opposite page: The crossroads at Overton.

of the De La Rue paper mill can be glimpsed above the tree line. Industry came early to the Test Valley with its many mills and more notably with Henri Portal's paper mill near Laverstock, which gradually expanded into the large enterprise it is today.

Quidhampton mill is now a charming redbrick private residence, although the turbulent waters of the mill race run noisily through the channel to hint at its industrial past. It became part of the Portal chain of mills along this stretch of the Test until the 20th century, and its origins stretch back to before Domesday, where the mill at Quidhampton was one of at least four operating in Overton. The others were the Town Mill, Lynch Mill (Later renamed as Southington) and Othin's Mill. This last mill was rebuilt c 1400 as a fulling mill. Fulling was an intensive process whereby all the impurities, such as natural oils and could be beaten out of woollen cloth. At first the process was undertaken by individuals using their hands and feet but the invention of the fulling mill in the middle ages, mechanised the process. At the fulling mill the wheel turned a system of cams which raised and lowered hammers onto the cloth, thereby beating out the unwanted elements, which could be washed away. Fuller's earth, a green sand,

was often used to chemically aid the process. In the 1600s Othin's Mill was converted to a corn mill and in the 18th century to a silk mill. The Portal family acquired the mill in 1813 and it closed as a working mill in 1846.

Overton

Overton is a large village of ancient importance, signified today by the crossroads at the heart of the village Medieval travellers would know of Overton. The ancient Portway from Silchester to Salisbury passed through it and from south to north travellers from Stockbridge to Basing would also meet at the crossroads. The village was granted a market in 1218

Southington Mill.. Above: Pickwick restaurant in Ovington.

which added much to its prosperity. The rights for additional fairs were granted in 1246 and 1519. The sheep fair, established in 1519 traded as many as 30,000 sheep. English wool was prized for its quality in medieval times and buyers came from as far away as Italy to make purchases Much was shipped from Southampton to Flanders, where they had the skills to turn wool into fine cloth.

Overton's sheep fairs were central to the economic prosperity of the manor and at one time there were as many as three each year. A century ago this number had dwindled to an annual fair held on July 18 where thousands of sheep were penned in the village. As the 20th century developed, such methods of selling livestock became unnecessary and the fair declined. It was recreated in 2000 as a Millennium celebration for the village. A flock of sheep was herded down Winchester Street to open the fair but this modern reincarnation was more about people than sheep.

In the 18th century a new industry emerged to compete with sheep farming – the manufacture of paper. The English had lagged behind their continental counterparts in the manufacture of paper, partly due to restrictions imposed by the Elizabethan government which feared that paper might be used to spread seditious pamphlets and it was not until the late 17th century that the government felt relaxed enough to give more permits to papermakers. Unfortunately, there were few native papermakers in the country with sufficient skill, so the arrival of Henri Portal, a Huguenot refugee from France, was doubly fortunate. He was able to attract a patron and develop a livelihood; paper making became a proper industry. Portal understood the technology and he arrived at a time when the government was willing to relax its restrictions on production. The higher reaches of the River Test proved to be ideal.

Henri Portal's new paper making business, which was established in 1710, brought a new industry to the area, which continues to this day with the de la Rue plant just to the north of Overton. However it was not until 1922 when Portals built a modern paper manufacturing plant just north of the town that the fortunes of the declining town were revived. Today Overton is a prosperous small town.

Overton's church lies to the north of the River Test, and is on the site of the original village. The new village, which is today the heart of present-

Ink and wash sketch of the river near Laverstoke.

day Overton, was laid on on a grid in the early 13th century. The church of St Mary dates dates from around 1180, although it is mainly a 13th century expansion and a late Victorian rebuild. It sits apart from the main village on a rise of land on the north bank.

One story that lingers from the 14th century tells of one John Bentley, who in 1390 arrived at Overton as a stranger. When questioned by the villagers he admitted that he had killed a man by accident and was seeking sanctuary. During a discussion in the churchyard, just inside the gate, a shoemaker by the name of Geoffrey gave him a hard shove so that he was outside the gate. Other villagers then set upon him and carried him to the stocks. On the following day he was taken to Winchester.

The villagers were technically not in violation of sanctuary, but bishop William of Wykeham took a dim view of their actions and ordered that John Bentley be restored to sanctuary. The final outcome of this story is unknown.

The White Hart Inn stands prominently at the cross roads and it is highly probable that there has been an inn on this site for at least 600 years. It was certainly a thriving establishment in 1516 when it was granted by Bishop Foxe of Winchester in 1521 to provide income for his new college, Corpus Christi, Shortly after this the inn was rebuilt and may have taken the form that is still recognisable today on the corner. During the great age of coaching in the 18th century a central arch would have allowed carriages with sprung wheels to pass under. The railway age, which for Overton began in 1840 with the opening of the London to Southampton line, pushed the coaching trade into decline. Once the London to Exeter railway opened 1854, coach traffic fell to nothing, as had been the experience in the rest of the country. Overton's importance was dwindling. Bradshaw's guide, recently revived by Michael Portillo, rather wearily comments that "Overton, an old dilapidated borough . . .has lost its Charter and Market and is chiefly and almost only attractive to the fisherman for the trout of the little stream."

The central archway into the yard was walled in to create more room space, as indeed was common with many former coaching inns, as early 20th century photographs show.

Henri de Portal came from a Huguenot family living at Poitiers. The Huguenots were French protestants whose reformed church was founded in the middle of the 16th century. They

Below: The compact church of St. Mary's at Laverstoke. Below: Bere Mill, Henri Portal's first mill on the Test.

had to bear long periods of persecution and the matter appeared to be resolved by the Edict of Nantes in 1643, where Huguenots were allowed some rights. The Edict was revoked in 1685. Shortly after this, Henri was born, circa 1690, and the fate of Huguenots became increasingly precarious. Henri and his brother Guillaume were sent to England, smuggled in wine barrels, so the story goes, and arrived in Southampton.

We know that Henri was employed at a paper mill at South Stoneham in 1710 and that in 1711 he was naturalised as a British subject. In 1712 he took out a lease on Bere Mill, just north of Whitchurch, and from this modest beginning the Portal paper making business grew rapidly. He was fortunate in the early period to have gained the friendship of Sir William Heathcote of Hursley, who was presumably able to guarantee the finances of the young Portal. By 1718 he took out a lease on Laverstoke Mill, which, as it developed and expanded, became the centre of the Portal empire for 200 years.

It was something of a coup for Henri to secure a deal with the Bank of England to make their banknotes. It was probably no accident that Sir Gilbert Heathcote, Governor of the Bank of England, was the uncle of Sir William Heathcote.

Bere Mill had only just been built when Henri Portal took out his lease, because only two years before, in 1710, the mill had been rebuilt for Jane Deane, the widow of Thomas Deane. She may have concluded that he was better off leasing the building to a miller than operating it herself. Bere Mill, surprisingly, has largely held on to its original features. It is now a private residence that stretches over a broad mill pond. The mill could have become redundant after the Laverstoke Mill grew in size and scope, but the Portals found a secondary use for the old mill. In 1904 they installed a turbine to produce electricity, which was then connected by cable to the Laverstoke Mill for its use. The Portal family way also retained a sentimental attachment to this mill, essentially the foundation of their larger paper making empire, otherwise its fate may have become that of many small 18th century mills — destruction.

The Laverstoke Mill grew and developed over the centuries but in the 20th century, when water power was no longer essential, a new plant was built north of Overton in 1922. The company remained under family control until 1995 when it was purchased by the de la Rue company. The Laverstoke Mill by this time was used mainly for administrative function. It is now owned by the Bombay Gin Company.

Henri Portal died on 30 September 1747 and is buried at the parish church in Whitchurch.

One of the recent arrivals to the River Test is the Bombay Gin distillery. I doubt whether the crystal clear quality of the Test's flowing waters had anything to do with that decision, but it does seem appropriate that a glass clear alcoholic liquid should be manufactured beside the naturally transparent waters of the river. Like several other Hampshire streams that flow to the sea the River Test is a chalk stream, that is, it flows rapidly over a bed of chalk in its downward progress. The properties of chalk, being porous and soluble in acid, means that water sinks into the ground while it flows over the chalk pebbles. Consequently the streams are never deep and unlike most rivers, the water contains few suspended particles. The river bed is always clearly visible, as are the fish that swim through these pristine waters.

A decade or so ago I was given permission to visit the Laverstoke mill.

Laverstoke village essentially grew

around the paper mill. In 1759, Portals

Part of the 19th century paper mill at Laverstoke. It is now the property of the Bombay Gin Distillery.

purchased the manor. The park today has a great mansion house and covers about 275 acres. This was constructed between the years 1796–1798.

The original parish church was dedicated to St Mary and was a modest building. It was annexed by the Portal family as their own private chapel. Laverstoke and Freefolk have three churches between them. The old church of St Mary's lies in the ground of Laverstoke Park and is now a ruin. A newer church, also dedicated to St

14

Mary, was built in 1896 of flint and brown stone. In a field off the beaten track at Freefolk is the church of St Nicholas, now used only occasionally. It is probably of 13ᵗʰ century origin although it is a very simple rectangular building.

Freefolk was a small underpopulated manor that included Bere Mill. The Portal family purchased the manor in 1769 and it remained largely undeveloped. Apart from a remote church in a field and a row of thatched roof cottages built for mill workers little else distinguishes the village. The row of cottages, built in the 20ᵗʰ century, actually in 1939, in a half-timbered style lie along the main road.

The overall effect (as may have been intended) is somewhat 'chocolate-boxy', with a sweeping thatched roof on a curve, landscaped cottage gardens, and a roofed well.

Almshouses at Freefolk

Below: The disused wheel of the old Whitchurch Town Mill.

The centre of Whitchurch. Below: Whitchurch Silk Mill.

Whitchurch

Five Roads meet at Whitchurch, although on some days you can stand at these crossroads and not encounter much traffic. The Winchester to Newbury road now bypasses the village on the A34 and the Basingstoke to Andover traffic is absorbed by the A303. The fifth road at this corners a north west country road. Whitchurch today is therefore a very quiet and peaceful village but it is evident from its architecture that it was once more important.

The White Hart Inn still impressively commands the corner and on Newbury Street is an impressive 18th century Town Hall.

Whitchurch's most famous native of recent time was the distinguished justice Lord Denning. He was born Alfred Thompson Denning on 23 January 1899 in Whitchurch. His father, Charles, ran a drapery business on Newbury Street. He was exceptionally bright and won several scholarships to Magdalen College, Oxford, where he eventually, with some interruption for war service, graduated in 1920 with a first class degree in Mathematics.

He taught mathematics for a period at Winchester College but found the work unsatisfying and turned his attention to law, returning to Magdalen in 1921 for further study. Over the next two decades he was increasingly sought after as a barrister and in 1944 was appointed to the High Court and knighted. He had a very distinguished career as a justice and was promoted to the highest offices. He was rightly celebrated for the clarity and elegance of his prose and regarded by some as the greatest English judge of modern times. Later in his life, his more conservative approach to morality left him out of step with the age he found himself living in. He resigned as Master of the Rolls in 1982.

On retirement he returned to his native Whitchurch and lived to pass his 100th birthday. On March 5th 1999 he was rushed to the RCH at Southampton, where he died of an internal haemorrhage.

The Whitchurch Silk Mill was originally built as a fulling mill in 1800 but was converted to a silk mill in 1817 by a new owner, Henry Hayter who then sold it two years later to William Maddick a London silk manufacturer and it was he who was largely responsible for developing the mill during his 30 year tenure.. The mill was successful and remained commercially viable until the second half of the 20th century. Operations

closed in 1985 and the property was acquired by the Hampshire Buildings Preservation Trust. It was opened to the public in 1990. In 2012, the Whitchurch Silk Mill Trust, which leases the premises, began to produce silk once again. They sell to specialised markets and the revenue helps to maintain the property.

The former Town Mill and Fulling Mill are now private residences.

James Robertson Justice was a well-known character actor in the mid 20th century. He had a commanding voice and a robust figure and his spade-shaped beard was always instantly recognisable. His rather brusque delivery of his lines left the impression that he was a man whose bark was always worse than his bite and he usually brought a smile to the faces of those who watched his films. He became especially associated with the comic "Doctor" series of films throughout the 1950s and 1960, where he played the role of Sir Lancelot Spratt. After the war he purchased the Lower Mill in Whitchurch as a home for himself, his wife and young son, James, who was born in 1945. Tragically, his son was drowned in the stream on 20th June 1949. The newspapers of the day offer no details but it is assumed that the four year old boy fell into the water.

The church, dedicated to All Hallows, was like many churches in the area, rebuilt in Victorian times although it still contains some 13th century elements. Its longer connection to antiquity is a Saxon period tomb which was uncovered during the restoration. It is inscribed "His corpus Frithbergae requiescet in pacem septum" – this body of Frithberga rests in peace. It has been suggested that the tomb dates from the 8th century. Frithberga was obviously a woman of some importance and it has been suggested that she was an abbess at Wherwell, but quite why her tomb should be found in Whitchurch is hard to explain, unless it was transferred after the dissolution. Nevertheless it is visible evidence of Whitchurch's ancient importance.

Above: The imposing Whitchurch Silk Mill.

Page 20: A pair of swans glliding downstream at Whitchurch..

Pages 16-17: The old railway bridge at Tufton.

The village of Tufton, which still retains a telephone box and a Victorian letter box.

Tufton

Tufton is a very small, isolated village about 2 miles to the south of Whitchurch. It lies at the end of an access road that reaches a dead end beside the river. I didn't count the number of buildings in the village, but I imagine it would not take much time. There is much of interest here. The church dates to the 12th century and has a pleasant location in the centre of the village on some higher ground. Inside is a painting of St Christopher that dates to the 14th century. Embedded in the wall surrounding the churchyard is a Victorian Post Box, at least 120 years old, I would think, and still in service. The villagers have also managed to hold to their telephone box. You will not be able to make a telephone call from here, but if you are short of reading material or need access to a defibrillator, then open the door of this sturdy piece of functional architecture.

The river widens at Tufton and pushes water along at a great rate, and just to the south of the village is another relic of a past age – a railway bridge. The railway has been long dismantled, but the bridge makes a splendid arch across the river.

See the painting on pages 16–17.

Bourne

A little to the south west of Tufton the Test is joined by its first tributary, the Bourne. This short valley, which includes the village of Hurstbourne Tarrant and St Mary Bourne, starts as the River Swift and then joins the Bourne south east of Hurstbourne Tarrant. The valley here has fairly steep sides and was apparently a favourite place of the 19th century traveller William Cobbett. In the 20th century, the valley gained some reflected glory when Harry Plunket Greene chose to live at Hurstbourne Priors. Plunkett Greene achieved fame as a bass-baritone singer in the late Victorian period and the Edwardian age. He was much admired, and performed song recitals to packed audiences in the era before radio and sound recordings.

He was born in Ireland in 1865, ten days after the poet William Butler Yeats. They both lived long lives, dying within three years of each other in the 1930s. Both were born into the Irish establishment; both men achieved high recognition for their art. There the parallels end. Yeats was political and pursued his passion for Irish nationalism; Plunket Greene was content to spend his adult life in England free of political controversy.

"Where bright waters meet."

His talent was first noticed in 1888 when he performed Handel's Messiah in London and he was in demand thereafter. He worked with Sir Hubert Parry and through him met his youngest daughter Gwendolen, whom he married in 1899. They had three children, all of whom were baptised in St Andrew's Church in Hurstbourne Priors. His singing career was enhanced by songs written for him by several the leading English composers of the day: Parry, Stanford, Elgar and Vaughn Williams. In his fifties he taught as a professor at the Royal College of Music and the Royal Academy of Music.

In 1902 he rented a house in the remote Hampshire village of Hurstbourne Priors. He was a very keen fly fisherman and he wrote about his experiences in a book published in 1924, "Where Bright Waters Meet." The book is now regarded as a classic book about the art of fishing, and Plunket Greene is probably in the same league as that other famous Hampshire fisherman, Izaak Walton. Plunket Greene writes in a humorous, self-deprecating way and has a talent for story telling. The book also tells us about a world that has since vanished.

He died on August 19th 1936 and is buried in Hurstbourne Priors.

Hurstbourne Park once had a huge stately home, a vast establishment according to an old engraving. It was demolished in 1891 and replaced by a late Victorian building in the Jacobean style. This too was demolished in 1965 after a fire and was replaced by a more modest, but still impressive building.

Longparish

As the name suggests, this parish straggles along the river for a mile or two. The B3048 is narrow and unhurried and at one point goes around three sides of a field, having no right of way over private land. This is still mill country and there is an upper mill and a lower mill. The upper mill is a private residence with some industrial buildings and is in a very attractive setting. The lower mills similarly arranged but with larger storage buildings dating from the 19th century.

The village has a kind of centre at the north end with a pub and village store. There is also a 20th century housing estate behind the road.

Somewhere in the middle of this long stretch, at the appropriately named Middleton, is the parish church of St Nicholas, a favourite name in these parts. The nave of the church dates from the early 13th century and the tower is later. Two village halls

Part of the Lower Mill at Longparish, largely surrounded by trees, offers an impressive sight as the weir spills into the main stream. The painting started from sketches and was completed in the studio as an oil painting,

and a primary school are also clustered in this centre. The Plough Inn which I sketched one Autumn when is was covered with red ivy, appears to have suffered the fate of many pubs and is now closed.

The road from Tufton to Longparish on the south east side of the river is probably the more attractive course to take. There is hardly any traffic on the road and is stays closer to the river. The road is known as Nuns Walk, possibly a hangover from days when Longparish was a property of Wherwell Abbey. There is a deepish ford that crosses the stream close to Longparish but I suspect that is is rarely used as there is better access on the other side.

Here is an interesting story from 1000 years ago. King Edgar, not a man known for high moral standards, heard of a great beauty from these parts by the name of Elfrida and he sent Earl Ethelwold to woo her on his behalf. Ethelwold, so the story goes, was so entranced by her beauty that he sent word back to Edgar that she was very plain looking and married her himself. That strategy unravelled when Edgar later paid a visit to hunt in Harewood forest and discovered that he had been deceived. While out hunting a day or two later he shot

On this page and on page 30, thatched cottages at Wherwell.

Ethelwold in the back and claimed Elfrida as his third wife. The year was 965

Elfrida seems to have been a willing participant in this plot to do away with her husband and her subsequent behaviour revealed a ruthless streak. She had one son by Edgar, who already had a son by his first wife, Ethelfleda. This son, Edward, succeeded his father in 975 but was murdered at Corfe Castle three years later, probably at the instigation of Elfrida. Leaving the way clear for her own son Ethelred. He was the one who became infamous as 'Ethelred the Unready', better translated as the one who would not heed advice rather than being unprepared. The old comes from the Anglo-Saxon "redeless."

What can be believed from this story is that Edgar and Ethelfreda got rid of the inconvenient husband. The part about Ethelwold betraying the king's trust may have been invented after the fact to excuse the murder.

Today you can see a monument to this story, a cross, which was erected in 1825 By Liutenenant Colonel William Iremonger. It became known as "Dead Man's Plack" which is a corruption of the name of the field in which it stands – "Dudman's Platt (Plot)"

Wherwell

This story has further associations with the area, because Ethelfleda, in penance for the murder of her stepson, founded and endowed the nunnery of Wherwell.

Wherwell is an attractive village with a number of thatched cottages on either side of the river, Some, while I was there on one visit, had recently succumbed to the risk of fire and were being rebuilt.

The village grew from the Benedictine nunnery that was established in the 10th century. It was well endowed and grew to be quite prosperous before it was dissolved in 1538.

Little evidence of it remains today. In fact, despite the village's quaint appearance, there is almost no trace of medieval Wherwell. The only clues can be found inside the 19th century church which contains fragments only of an earlier church. The mansion house, known as the Priory is also early 19th century.

The abbey was founded, as we have mentioned, by Queen Elfrida, after some remorse about her earlier crimes, or more likely through fear for her immortal soul, and some legendary tales attached to the place. Some say

that the place is haunted by evil spirits waiting to drag the tormented ghost of Elfrida down to the depths of hell.

Another story tells of a duck which laid an egg in a vault beneath the abbey. A toad sat on the egg and in consequence a cockatrice hatched out. A cockatrice was one of those fanciful medieval monsters, essentially a two-legged dragon with a rooster's head. This beast grew to a great size in the vault and killed any living thing that went down there. Eventually someone hit upon the idea of taking a mirror down into the vault, whereupon the cockatrice saw an image of itself and wore itself out attacking the mirror. Once the monster had worn itself out a man went own into the vault and dispatched it.

As a consequence there was always a superstition in Wherwell about eating duck's eggs and they were avoided. I doubt if the superstition prevails today.

When it came to the dissolution in the 1530s there was a great deal of underhand activity to get to control the prize. The abbey had been valued at £403 12s 10d in 1535 which made it one of the desirable plums. It had moreover, an unsullied reputation. There was no evidence of financial mismanagement or loose living which could be used to justify the closure.

In the end, the abbess was persuaded to accept a very generous pension of £20 a year and a new compliant abbess Morphita Kingsmill was brought in. It appears that the intention was to grant the house to John Kingsmill, brother of the abbess, but at the 11th hour Thomas West, Lord de la Warre made vigorous representations to Cromwell that he should be entitled to it as his own lands adjoined the abbey. Cromwell agreed and de la Warre got possession. Abess Kingsmill was given the very generous pension of £40 a year, which, at a time when an average family was getting by on £5 a year, made her very well-off.

The River Dever rises to west of Micheldever, close to the old Roman road that went from Winchester to Basingstoke. The stream joins the Test near Wherwell. Above it, a mile and a half from the main river lies the village of Barton Stacey. Today, it is unremarkable, but for what happened over 200 years ago. The village was destroyed by a fire in 1792, which started in a blacksmith forge. The fire on the thatched roof was carried to similarly roofed cottages and almost nothing survived the inferno. For entirely understandable reason, residents have resisted the temptation to thatch their roofs, and, unlike similar Hampshire villages, there are none to be found there today. The rebuilding

Thatched cottages are plentiful in Abbots Ann, and indeed are common enough in the upper reaches of the Test Valley.

program after 1792 provided some buildings from the late 18th century, such as the house that now serves as the Village Stores, but most of the buildings date from after the 1930s.

The River Dever runs as a modest stream nearby and feeds into the Test. There is a trout fishery here.

Anna Valley

Below Wherwell, two more streams, the River Ann and the River Anton, join and flow into the Test. They are worth a detour.

The villages bordering the Ann river have become a thatchers paradise. The thatchers craft was dying 60 years ago but new cottage owners, able to earn their income outside the village, saw to it that thatched roofs were properly installed and maintained, and in some cases newly installed. The villages present a picturesque face to the world along their main streets with some older, timber-framed cottages leaving visible reminders of earlier building practices.

Abbots Ann is now a largish village with over a quarter of its houses built in the past 25 years, nevertheless significant buildings survive from the 19th century and earlier. The church of St Mary was built by Thomas "Diamond" Pitt who made a fortune in

This curious collection of 20th century memorabilia is on display at a house in Abbots Ann

India. The church is now 300 years old.

Thomas Pitt was born in Blandford Forum in 1653, the son of John Pitt, the rector of Blandford St Mary. At the age of 21 he joined the East India Company but quickly saw the possibilities of trading for himself. In consequence he quickly became rich and powerful. At home he was able to buy the manor that included Old Sarum, a depopulated castle which was still entitled to provide a member of Parliament. That MP was naturally Thomas Pitt.

By the end of the 17th century he had become Governor of Madras and essentially ruled that province for the East India Company. In England he was able to buy a number of manors including Abbots Ann, where he rebuilt the church in 1716. He died

Left: An arch leading to St Mary's Church, Andover.

Below: An ivy covered pub at Longparish - now closed.

Bottom: The Crook and Shears at Clatford.

On page 36: A sketch of Andover Town Hall and below - Fullerton Mill.

at Swallowfield Park in Berkshire in 1726.

He purchased a 410 carat diamond (uncut) in 1701. He paid £20,400 for it and after it was cut and polished it was sold to Phillipe II, Duc de Orleans for £135,000. The diamond became one of the French crown jewels and is today on display at the Louvre.

His descendants went on to greater fame. His grandson, William Pitt, became Prime Minister and was created Earl Chatham. His great-grandson, William Pitt the younger, achieved the office of Prime Minister at the early age of 24 and held the office for a total of 19 years. He is rated as one of our greatest Prime Ministers.

As the name of the village suggests the manor was once the property of an abbot, in this case the Abbot of New Minster in Winchester, later known as Hyde Abbey. This association came to an end during the general dissolution of the monasteries after 1536.

The Anna river, a short stream, now carries the name of Pillhill Brook, enters the River Anton at Upper Clatford.

Anton Valley

The river Anton is fed by springs to the north of Andover and is channeled through the town. South of Andover it passes through the Clatfords and joins the main test river just south of Fullerton. Like its big sister it is a chalk stream of very clear water and is highly prized by fly fishers.

At the head of the river, Andover, once a small market town, grew voraciously to a large urban sprawl over the past 50 years, much like Basingstoke. Andover was historically a large manor, extending over 8000 acres. Much of that has been developed in the last century.

It was always a royal manor, pre-dating the Conquest even, but successive kings showed little interest in it and no royal castles or palaces were ever built here. It held some importance as a stopping place on the high road west of London and in the 19th century hosted the main line railway.

The parish church of St Mary's is a prominent feature and a most impressive building, built on the high point above the town. The present church is completely Victorian and was built between 1840 and 1844 on the site of the medieval church, of which there are few remnants. The

cost of the building was borne by Dr Goddard, an 18th century headmaster of Winchester College, who retired in 1809 to Andover. The large churchyard surrounding it was once the site of a priory. It was granted by William the Conqueror to the Benedictine Priory of St Florent in Saumur in the Loire Valley and of course all its income went to the parent house. This was stopped in 1414 when Henry V dissolved the priory and granted it to Winchester College. Almost nothing remains of the priory today.

The old town is built around a large market square, dominated by a 19th century Town Hall, and indeed, almost all the buildings in this part of Andover date no further back than the early 19th century. Much of commercial Andover has been rebuilt to service the expanded population, although the core of the market square remains.

The small village of Upper Clatford, which stretches along a narrow road, would not immediately call to mind the Industrial Revolution, but here, admidst a collection of thatched cottages was the Waterloo Iron Works, established here in the year of that celebrated battle. It is difficult today to conceive of heavy industry in this rural backwater, conditioned as we are to vast northern and midland towns dominating industry

in the past, but nevertheless, the works were once here.

The iron works were established by Robert and William Tasker. They manufactured agricultural implements such as ploughs, and gates and domestic items such as cooking stoves. The Tasker brothers were able to benefit from cheap coke and iron, which could be hauled by barge from Southampton along the nearby canal.

The company did not survive into the next generation and almost nothing remains today to record its former presence, but for an iron bridge across the river Anton, built in 1843, is still in use today. The iron bridge is a flat span on Church Lane.

Bury Hill, about half a mile to the west along Red Rice Road, shows the earthworks of an iron age hill fort. It is a large circle surrounded by defensive earth banks.

The Mill House at Fullerton is a grade II listed building. It is on an ancient site with a house attached and originally dated from the late 1700s. Although not visible the cut-waters and race are intact and within the mill there remains a 19th century metal wheel.

On this page: Cottages at Chilbolton and the Church.

On page 39: The bridge at Testcombe and a weir at Leckford.

Longparish to Stockbridge

Chilbolton's village lies to the east of the river. Its church, with a rather squat wooden bell tower, capped with a spire, is dedicated to St Mary the Less. The origin of this curious name is unknown and may not refer to the character of St Mary. One suggestion is that the church itself was compared to the far larger church in Andover, and if so, its designation as "the less" would be accurate. The village is quiet and holds a number of thatched cottages which lend a picturesque appearance to the village.

two Test Way footpaths: one branching to Chilbolton and the other towards Fullerton

A more modern development is the radio telescope which was opened on the downs above Chilbolton in 1967.

Leckford is a small roadside village on the eastern bank of the river, with a population of just over 100. The road runs alongside the old railway line, which is now used as the test Way footpaths. The village gives its name to the Leckford estate, which grows produce for Waitrose stores across the country.

Slightly below it at Testcombe is the attractive riverside pub and restaurant called The Mayfly. Just below, the River Anton flows into the Test and the river begins to widen into separate streams as the valley opens up. The road bridge spans both the river and the abandoned railway bridge crosses the river here. This is also a junction of

Features in the village are the church and village stores, and a row of half-timbered, thatched cottages.. The church, dedicated to St Nicholas, is a low height building dating to the 13th century, and was last modified in the 16th century

There is one large house here, known as Abbass Grange, now, as so much in these parts, owned by the John

The river at Longparish.

On page 41: Water Gardens at longstock. Longstock House and Sundial in the gardens.

Lewis Partnership. The house at the centre of the old manorial estate that was once the property of St Mary's

Abbey, Winchester. The house has the appearance of a late Elizabethan or 17th century mansion, but it is in reality a 20th century building created in the older style.

The Leckford estate extends across the river and includes Longstock. Longstock House was acquired by John Lewis in 1946 and is now at the heart, in more ways than one, of the John Lewis empire.

John Lewis was an original thinker who was a businessman ahead of his time. He reasoned that a happy employee was likely to be a more productive employee. So he set about introducing better working conditions through shorter working days and extended holidays. In the early 20th century the prevailing culture in the retail trade was that the employees were servants

and were often treated no better than domestic servants. After about 20 year the idea of each employee being a partner in the organisation evolved and the unique John Lewis Partnership was created.

First, and largely invisible to the casual viewer, is a 4000 acre

A view from Danebury

farm which is a serious agricultural enterprise supplying the Waitrose chain of supermarkets. Part of the estate is set aside for leisure facilities for staff of the John Lewis Partnership. There are two 9 hole gold courses and the rights to fish on stretches of the River Test.

The water gardens were created around an artificial lake in the valley. One is reminded of Monet's diversion of the River Seine to create his famous lily pond. These gardens cover just over five acres and offer the visitor a visual treat in the Summer months. They are not open to the public every day, usually some Sundays in the Summer months.

Longstock House is available to employees for workshops and seminars.

Stockbridge

High above the river, with Stockbridge to the south east, is one of the most impressive iron age hill forts. Danebury was probably first built as a single rampart and ditch around 550BC. In subsequent years the rampart was raised several times and it was probably abandoned around 100BC. There is evidence of several farms from the period lower down the valley and it seems probable that the fort was a place to find safety when the district was under threat.

The broad main street of Stockbridge is its defining characteristic. It stretches from east to west for about half a mile over the wide bed of the valley. Flat bridges cross several streams which were possibly dug for flood control at one time. In the last century this road bore dense traffic to the west country through Salisbury, but the building of the A303 has turned Stockbridge into a quiet town.

Conventional High Street shops steer clear of places like Stockbridge, so most of the shops along the street, apart from those that deal in essentials, are occupied by art galleries and craft shops, which makes the town an interesting place for a leisurely visit.

The main church is late Victorian, although there is an older 13th century nave, the remnant of a medieval church within the church yard. This is known as "Old St Peters".

As the name of the town suggests this was a road for drovers and the settlement grew around the bridge, which presumably exacted tolls from the drovers of sheep and cattle and geese.

The town hall, in yellow brick, dates from 1810 and was apparently offered as a bribe to the voters. Stockbridge

Stockbridge: A view from the meadow. Below: the main street.

On page 45: The Woodfire Restaurant, formerly Stokes Garage.

had a somewhat disreputable history in Parliamentary elections. With a small number of eligible voters bribery was relatively simple and was done openly in the 17th and pat of the 18th centuries. As disgust at this practice increased, prospective MPs became more sophisticated in their offerings to the voters and the Town Hall was an example of this. The seat returned two MPs even though it had a small population and one seat was sold to Earl Grosvenor in the early 19th century for one of his nominees. The Stockbridge seat disappeared after the Reform Act of 1832 and became part of a northern Hampshire constituency.

The Grosvenor Hotel juts out into the High Street with a large semi circular room supported by columns for the porch entrance.

Further west is a house that was once the home of the celebrated Victorian beauty, Lily Langtry. For many years in the 20th century it was Stokes garage and outside the building today you can see an old early 20th century petrol pump, dating from the time when this was a busy thoroughfare. The building is now a restaurant.

Above: The White Hart at Kings Somborne.

Below: The renovated railway station at Horsebridge.

Kings Somborne

As the name might suggest, King's Somborne was originally a royal manor. However, it was not known as King's Somborne at that time. A series of inheritances brought it back into royal hands at the end of the 14th century. It was granted to William Brewer in 1190. In the 14th century it came into the hands of Henry Grossmont, earl of Lancaster and eventually passed through marriage to John of Gaunt, who himself became Duke of Lancaster. His eldest son, Henry, inherited in 1399, but almost immediately after launched a successful coup against Richard II and became King Henry IV. The duchy of Lancaster was then, and has been ever since, a crown estate. So once again Somborne became Kings Somborne.

The estate itself was large and occupies most of the eastern side of the valley between Romsey and Stockbridge.

The village still has some remains of an old palace. Locally it is known as King John's palace, but it is unlikely that King John had anything to do with the place. More plausible is that the palace was built in the time of John of Gaunt in the 14th century. There is a documentary reference in 1362 when it was granted to John of Gaunt's wife. There are two buildings on the site – Old Palace Lodge and Palace Farmhouse. The farmhouse has been converted to two residences. The basis of the building is 16th century, but there is evidence of modification and rebuilding in every century since.

Horsebridge amounts to a mill, a pub named after the former landowner, John of Gaunt, a few cottages, and an old railway station. This last building is probably the most interesting. The Sprat and Winkle line, which ran from Romsey to Andover, built a station here and when it was closed in 1962. Twenty or so years later Anthony and Valerie Charrington had the foresight to purchase the building and land and as a private residence, and spent a good deal of time and money restoring the derelict buildings. It is now a wedding venue. The station building still shows off its Victorian heritage and all the paintwork is in the livery of the old Southern Railway – green.

Houghton

The road from Stockbridge on the west bank of the Test lies closer to the river and passes through the elongated village of Houghton and then to Bossington. Many old buildings have stood the test of time, including one which has 15th century timbers.

Houghton Lodge is a strange building.

It was constructed at the turn of the 19th century and deliberately designed to look like a country cottage. The style was known as "cottage ornée". In consequence the house is not high and imposing and appears like a 1 1/2 storey building with the upper floor in the roof. The gardens are open to the public.

The Boot Inn is built in a half timbered style but it looks very much 20th century and was probably converted from a row of cottages, The church of All Saints, just up Church Lane, has low walls and a steep rake for the tiled roof. It has a low tower capped with a wooden spire.

Broughton

A further detour to the west takes us to the village of Broughton, and there is much of interest here.

The churchyard has a dovecote surviving from the 17th century. It is a small round brick building with a turret roof. Openings in the louver offer access for the birds. There are 482 nesting boxes built into the walls, although I have not counted them.

At the corner of Plough Gardens and the High Street is a heavy timber open structure that could be mistaken for a bus shelter. It is known as the Well House and was designed to cover

the village well. It was donated to the village by J T Fripp in 1926.

Broughton has some older timber framed cottages but many are 19th and 20th century brick

The church of St Mary contains some elements from c 1200, but most of the structure, with a solid tower, was built or rebuilt in the late 14th or early 15th century.

Dovecote at Broughton. Dovecotes were built in England after the Norman Conquest in 1066 and remained structures for the privilehed until the 18th century. They were primarily a source of meat.

On the left hand page: a weir along the river.

49

Fishing

The Test is famed for its fishing, in particular the art of fly fishing. The Houghton Fishing Club was founded in 1822 and is the oldest such club in the world. Initially there were 13 members; today the number is limited to only 25. Meetings are held at the Grosvenor Hotel in Stockbridge.

Fishing is tightly regulated. Seasons are limited and the use of worms is prohibited. The banks and the fishing rights are privately owned. The middle and upper reaches are valued for trout fishing and the lower reach, below Romsey can be fished in season for migratory salmon and sea trout.

Palmerston's statue in Romsey Square. Below: 17th century half-timbered building.

Romsey

As an old town Romsey has much appeal. The main square, with a statue of the great Lord Palmerston in the centre, is surrounded by a mixture of 18th and 19th century buildings. The square is closer to a triangle than a four-sided space, but there are fours streets radiating from it – Church St, to the north, The Hundred to the south east, Bell street going south and The Abbey to the west. Most are full of buildings and shops of some interest.

On the west side is a stylish brick building in Lloyds Bank style, now a TSB bank. Next to it is an impressive Georgian town house, which for many years was a chemist's. The 19th century town hall stands at the head of Bell street. In fact, most of Romsey's prominent buildings are Victorian; the Town Hall was built in 1866, the Corn Exchange, currently Barclay's Bank, 1864, and the Congregational Church, next to the abbey with a flintstone rendering, was built in 1887-8. At one end of Palmerston Street stands a timber framed building of two gables. The timbers are in-filled with brick nogs. Next door is another gable roofed building which may, judging by the weight of the timbers, be somewhat older. The house has been rendered and painted white.

The abbey is still an impressive building, although it has lost its cloisters. The great tower of the former abbey still rises over all of the town's buildings and for about six centuries the Benedictine nunnery held sway over the town. The present building was built in the time of Henry of Blois, bishop of Winchester, on the old Saxon foundations. One visible Saxon element survives, a stone cross carved into the wall on the south side. Inside, the stone columns of the aisle and the rounded arches reveal it Norman origins. In the 13th century the abbey supported over 100 nuns and it was one of the greater foundations in Hampshire. The Black Death of 1348-9 was catastrophic and 72 nuns died in this period as well as 500 townsfolk.

The abbey never fully recovered its former standing and there was even scandal in the late 15th century when it was discovered that one of the male chaplains was pimping the services of some of the nuns to townsmen. The abbey was supressed in 1539. The building was somewhat lucky. Whereas many former religious houses were converted to large houses or, like Hyde and Wherwell, demolished, the townspeople of Romsey came forward and offered to purchase the property as a parish church. The request was

Sadler's Mill. Below: Romsey Abbey

granted and £100 changed hands. The part of the building which had up to that point served as a parish church, was demolished, and the abbey church took its place. The cloisters were later removed.

South of the town lies the Palmerson estate of Broadlands, occupied by the Mountbatten family from the 20th century.

Viscount Palmerston was one of those larger-than-life characters thrown up by the 19th century. He entered politics as a Tory MP in 1807 and achieved cabinet status in his late 30s. He served as Foreign secretary on three occasions over a twenty year period, and it is as a robust interventionist in foreign conflicts that he is best remembered. His interventionist approach was criticised at the time as being risky, but on the whole, his policy worked and his rampant nationalism enjoyed wide public support. He was twice Prime Minister, from 1855–1858 and from 1859–1865 and he died in office in 1865.

He switched political parties in 1830, joining the Whigs, which later morphed into the Liberal Party. This was still an age where changing parties did no lasting damage to one's career.

His reputation as Foreign Secretary remains high. He averted the secession of Belgium to France by supporting the idea of an independent country. He opposed Austrian control over the Savoyard kingdom of Northern Italy, and the drive for Italian unification and independence. In both these instances, Palmerston's influence has been long lasting.

The Broadlands estate was acquired by Palmerston's father in the 18th century and "Capability" Brown was commissioned to undertake some work there. Viscount Palmerston typically used it as a country retreat. It is now in the hands of the Mountbatten family.

For a pleasant walk out to the river meadows, take The Abbey from the Market Square to the west. This runs into The Meads. Follow this road over one channel of the Test, north of the park, to Sadlers Mill. A footbridge crosses the fast-running streams, which incorporates a salmon leap. The road called The Causeway follows the west bank of the river to the main road. Turn east over the bridge and join Middlebridge Street. At the end of that street you can join Bell Street and return to the square.

Across the street from the Abbey is a 13th century house, one of the oldest in the country. It is popularly known as King John's House after it was enthusiastically identified by a

local historian as a hunting lodge used by King John. More recent, scientific dendron-dating places the origins of the building much later in the century and certainly well after the death of King John in 1217. The actual purpose of the original building is unknown but it is conjectured that it may have been used a a guest house for visitors to the abbey. For those who cling to the idea that it was used by King John, it is possible that a building was first erected during the time of King John and was then replaced 40 years later. It was certainly under royal control because Henry III granted it to the Abbey for use as an extra-mural guest house for the abbey.

The narrow, two story building, with its uneven floors and medieval beams with exposed carpenter's marks, is now a heritage centre.

Romsey keeps changing. This drawing was made 20 years ago. Top left: The former Lloyds Bank. Bottom left: King John's House.

Mottisfont Abbey. Below: St Andrew, Mottidfont.

Mottisfont

William Brewer left a large footprint on Hampshire. He was a senior member of government in the reigns of Richard I, John and his son Henry III and was suitably rewarded with lands in Hampshire and Devon. He founded Mottisfont Priory in 1201 for monks of the Augustinian order. Mottisfont itself, as the name suggests, was a fertile settlement with a ready source of spring water. The district became an important enough centre to hold courts (moots) there. The priory was well-endowed and prospered until the Black Death when the inmates were decimated. After this, in common with many other institutions, it struggled.

The priory came under the sway of Henry of Lancaster and subsequently to his son in law John of Gaunt. In the 15th century, as part of the duchy of Lancaster, Henry VI petitioned for the house to be dissolved to support his new college at Eton. However, although permission was given, the order was never implemented and the house limped along until the general dissolution of 1536. After which is was granted to William Sandys, chamberlain to Henry VIII. He converted it into a country home, keeping the church nave as the main hall with new wings built on either side. The cloisters were also retained.

New owners in the 18th century, the Mill family, undertook some major remodelling. The cloisters were torn down and the frontage of the house was given a more modern appearance. The place was henceforth known as Mottisfont Abbey.

The original medieval church is still in evidence, with the later additions built around them. You can also discover 13th-century cellarium.

In common with many great estates assembled in the 18th century, Mottisfont Abbey became a country retreat for such recreations as hunting, shooting and fishing. Towards the end of the 19th century the house was let to a wealthy banker, Daniel Meinertzhagen, who had no fewer than ten children, two of whom, Daniel and Richard, pursued a medieval passion for hawking. The two men built aviaries for a zoo of eagles, hawks, owls and ravens. Richard Meinertzhagen compiled detailed diaries about his birds, which are of interest to enthusiasts.

In 1934 another banker came to the 2000 acre estate, Gilbert Russell, from a cadet branch of the Russell dukes of Bedford. His wife, Maud, was an art connoisseur, and as a well-connected family, she was able to build a coterie of leading politicians,

Barn at Lee. Below: Fishing bat Longridge

aristocrats, artists and writers

She formed a romantic attachment with Ian Fleming at about this time and remained close to him. She stumped up £5000 so that he could buy the land and build his house called Goldeneye on the coast of Jamaica. The artist Ben Nicholson was also a frequent visitor and she commissioned Rex Whistler, with whom she also had an affair, to paint a trompe l'oeil gothic interior in one of the rooms – now known as the Whistler Room. Whistler skilfully created a three dimensional appearance of vaulted arches and carved embellishments, entirely on flat surfaces.

The Southampton painter, Derek Hill, was also a visitor. He mainly worked as a society portrait painter, but had a personal inclination to paint landscapes. Late in life he purchased old rectory in Churchill, County Donegal, which I visited some years ago The north west coast of Ireland formed the inspiration for many of his landscapes.

Mottisfont village is very tiny, but it does have an interesting church. Dedicated to St Andrew, it was built in the 12th century. Its glory is a three-panel stained glass window at the eastern end. The central panel depicts the crucifixion, while the supporting panels show St Andrew and St Peter. The panel was made in the 15th century and is believed to have come from the chapel of the Holy ghost in basingstoke. The design of the window seems to have been inspired by an earlier window in York Minster.

Estuary

The meadowlands below Romsey are generally underpopulated. Much of the land belongs to the Broadlands estate. A chapel at Lee has been converted to a venue for the Romsey Art Group and there is a mill at Nursling. West of the river lies the huge modern development of Totton and Testwood. There is also a large retail park beside the M271 at Nursling

There are not many working tide mills left in this country, but Eling Tide Mill is one of those few. The mill works on the principle that the water surges upstream during an incoming tide. In this part of the day a

The Old Bridge at Redbridge. Below: Eling Tide Mill.

sluice gate is opened and the reservoir behind the mill is filled. At low tide the water is allowed to escape through the water wheel, thus creating the power source. With Southampton's natural phenomenon of double tides, the Eling Tide Mill is able to operate much of the day.

A mill was recorded on the site in 1066 so it was most likely established much earlier. The present building dates from the late 18th century. It was a functioning flour mill until the 1940s, when it was abandoned. The mill was restored as a working mill and a heritage site between 1975 and 1980 and it is one of three fully working tide mills in the country. A single track causeway bridge collects tolls.

The church of St Mary the Virgin is very old and excavations discovered part of a 9th century (or earlier) Celtic cross, suggesting that the site had been used from the earliest days of christianity in England. dating back to the 9th (possibly the 6th) century was found. The site of St Mary's has been a place of Christian worship since that date. The present church was rebuilt in Victorian times but preserved some Norman and Saxon elements.

Redbridge is an ancient community mentioned in the Domesday Book, and it seems sensible that some sort of community would grow at a bridge crossing. The medieval bridge was about half a mile north of the later bridges, at a narrower crossing. The old stone bridge was built in the very early part of the 18th century by Redbridge merchants and presumably operated as a toll bridge. It was of the pack horse type, that is a very narrow bridge, with passing bays across the span. The bridge was later widened. As was the second bridge, originally built in 1793 to traverse a spot where another river channel had broken through. The old bridge survived in general use until 1930 when the new causeway was built. This bridge was doubled in the 1960s.

Part of the old village was demolished during the construction of the new bridge, but the Ship Inn, which was built in 1654, still stands.

And perhaps that name reminds us that Redbridge, although never a large community, was once an important shipbuilding centre. Timber was readily available from the New Forest, and new boats could be easily floated from the shore.

Now invisible, but once an early industrial feature in these parts, was the Andover Canal, that followed a course from Southampton Water along

View of Southampton from Hythe. Below: Docks on the Test estuary

the Test and Anton valleys to Andover. All that remains of the canal today is a course between Romsey and Timsbury, and a stretch beside the wharf in the town of Andover itself. The canal was completed in 1794 but was never commercially successful. In the 1840s, railway companies were interested in purchasing the canal in order to use the land to build a railway, and after some years of haggling, the canal was sold to create a railway from Redbridge to Andover, later nicknamed the 'Sprat and Winkle' line. Most of the course of the canal was used for the railway bed.

Construction began in 1859 and the line opened in 1865. Stations were built along the line at Nursling, Romsey, Mottisfont, Horsebridge, Stockbridge, Fullerton, Clatford and Andover. It was taken over by the London and South Western Railway in 1863 and the line formed junctions at Cambridge and Fullerton with other lines.

Apart from Andover and Romsey there were no towns of any significance along the line and in an age before commuting to work, there was little passenger traffic other than rural people going to the seaside. As a result it got the nickname of the Sprat and Winkle line.

The Sprat and Winkle line was later extended from Fullerton to join the main western line at Hurstbourne. It construction was motivated by the commercial politics of the day with perceived competition from the Didcot, Newbury and Southampton Railway, which was one of the later Victorian railways. In the ned neither line really profited, although it did open up Longparish to railway services. Long before Beeching the line was closed to passenger traffic in 1931 and partially to goods traffic in 1934. The Longparish to Fullerton junction section was kept open until 1956 because of the large sawmill at Longparish and, during WWII, to carry ammunition from a storage depot built at Longparish.

Due to the low volume of traffic the line was earmarked for closure by Dr Beeching. Passenger service was withdrawn on 7 September 1964 and goods traffic ceased after 18 September 19z67.

Some traces of the line remain. There is the station at Horsebridge and a derelict platform at Fullerton junction. Railway bridges survive at Horsebridge, Chilbolton, Fullerton, Tufton and Whitchurch.

The last two miles of the river are bordered by greater Southampton on the north side and some sparse settlements of the south side. Southampton will not be part of this book, but we can include Hythe, opposite Southampton. Hythe, as its name would suggest, is a harbour. While the great ships dock at Southampton, smaller boats, mostly pleasure craft, find a harbour on the edge of the New Forest. The marina is modern in design and construction. The frontage offers a good view of Southampton and its shipping.

There is easy access to Southampton across the water. A pier extends some distance into the estuary and a train shuttles back and forth from the mainland to the ferry point. The ferry operates at 30 minute intervals.

The town is mainly a 20th century development although the settlement goes back some distance in time. At the beginning of the 20th century it was little more than a fishing village.

The village of Marchwood, although of some antiquity, is now associated with heavy industry. There is a large electricity generating power station on the shore and a refuse incinerator. A military port was established here in the 1939-1945 war and this continues in use. The shore also hosts an industrial park.

The river joined the Itchen at Southampton itself and becomes Southampton Water. Technically speaking, it is part of the river, but it takes on a new character here, and this maybe a good point to end this little survey.

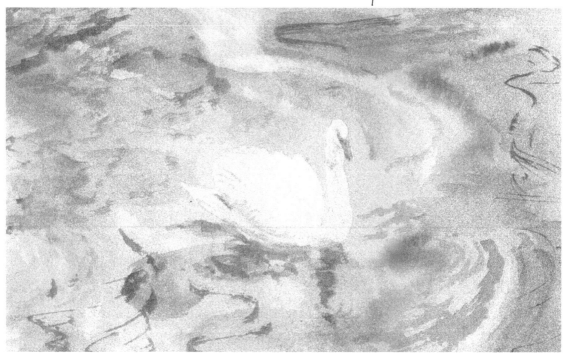

Meon: A Painter's Journey Down the River Valley.

ISBN: 978-1-909054-09-7

Puboished 2013   72 pages in full colour £9.99

Walking Winchester

Bryan Dunleavy and Olena Thomas

An illustrated guide to historic Winchester.

ISBN: 978-1-909054-24-0

Published 2014128 pages in full colour   £9.99.

London:An Artist's Exploration..

ISBN: 978-1-909054-31-8

Puboished 2013   72 pages in full colour £9.99

Some of the pictures illustrated here are available as original artworks. Some may be available as prints or used as images for greetings cards.

For further information go to www.magicfluteartworks.co.uk.

Magic Flute Publications

Publishers of books, cards and art prints. www.magicflutepublications.co.uk

Lightning Source UK Ltd.
Milton Keynes UK
UKHW05f2002290818
328000UK00003B/39/P